Dad's

100 Poems, Songs, and Riddles Within

Series 2

Jeffrey Krueger

ISBN: 979-8-9870661-4-0 - Hardcover
ISBN: 979-8-9870661-3-3 - Paperback
eISBN: 979-8-9870661-5-7 - eBook

Library of Congress Control Number: 2023919521

♾ This paper meets the requirements of ANSI/NISO Z39.48-1992 (Permanence of Paper)

060524

*Dedicated to
my father,
Roy Francis Krueger,
my wife, family, friends,
and all who donated to help families in need*

❧❦ **Acknowledgments** ❦❧

I don't believe I'd be alive right now to write anything if it wasn't for the grace and mercy of my Heavenly Father. I am so blessed and thankful for my wife and family who inspire me.

A renewed thanks for Bryan O., who listened and read every one of my poems in this second book. I also must give credit and a special appreciation to his wife, Janice, who proofed and helped me edit.

For all my family, friends, and others who made my first book successful by purchasing or donating to raise proceeds for the Family Needs Fund charity, helping families in need, a thankful and great shout-out to all of you.

My hope and desire are that this second book of Dad's 100 Poems, Songs, and Riddles Within *will give you joy, laughter, and some thoughtful contemplation.*

Contents

Introduction

After finishing my first book, Dad's 100 Poems, Riddles, and Songs in 100 Days, *I felt exhilaratingly compelled to continue my dad's legacy and complete a second book of* Dad's 100 Poems, Songs, and Riddles Within. *It was such a joy to be inspired in this creative endeavor to exercise my brain. Sounds a little crazy, but I can't imagine doing anything else with my extra time.*

I also wanted to further the mission of raising funds for families in need through the charity the Family Needs Fund. My third objective was to highlight my ability to overcome certain parts of my learning difference (dyslexic disorder), spelling, and writing incapabilities.

As the saying goes, I'm proof in the pudding. With determination and perseverance, you can accomplish almost anything you set your mind to. My accomplishments aren't as grand as sailing across the ocean or climbing to the top of Mount Everest. But in this creative process, I have discovered tremendous healing from certain childhood wounds as I express my thoughts and words on paper. These undertakings of writings felt as though I did sail across the ocean or have reached the top of Mount Everest. To be honest, I had extra help by God's Holy Spirit's guidance and grace.

On this adventure, I set sail to write 100 poems and songs at my leisure within one year: 2022. Completing 100 poems in 100 days became remarkably fluid. It was truly a gift to my self-esteem and brought some healing and quiet time with the Lord. I would have never thought in a million years I could write 100 poems in 100 days and another book of 100 poems. I'm not sure why 100 days or 100 poems, or why rhyming subjects.

I do know one thing—it brought me closer to my relationship with my Heavenly Father and gave me encouragement to understand more about who I am as God sees me. Hopefully, I can give that encouragement to others.

As explained in my first book, I haven't studied poetry. I have little or no teaching about poetry. I'm not aware of any authority that has critiqued my poems, riddles, or songs, so I haven't been influenced to change my inspired flow. I just dove back into the deep innocence and creative joy of writing stories and rhymes of simple, fun, silly, spiritual, and some complex subjects.

My hope and desire are that these 100 Poems, Songs, and Riddles Within *will bring some humor, enjoyment, and spiritual closeness, and will challenge some investigative pondering of what's being shared.*

All the proceeds from Dad's 100 Poems, Songs and Riddles Within *are given to the Family Needs Fund to help families in need.*

About the Poems, Riddles, and Songs

As I stated in the introduction, I wrote Dad's Poems, Songs, and Riddles Within *with a continued innocence and creative joy, continuing where I left off from my first book of poems. I liken it to an artist drawing sketches of things and subjects around them, eventually using those sketches to complete the final painting, or a guitarist playing their favorite song alone in their private space.*

I must admit I am totally energized and fully satisfied each time I sit down to write. It's like being filled up by a home-cooked meal, or sitting by a fire on a cold winter night, or feeling the wind against my face when crossing the lake, by boat, on a hot summer day. I get lost in this new-world adventure of creating story rhymes and experiencing a peaceful time with the Divine.

My adult children might compare it to standing in a deer stand waiting for the big buck, or casting out the fishing line to hook a the big one, playing hockey, planting and harvesting a garden, riding a horse bareback, or being captured by a good movie.

Each poem comes to me on any given day. Some subjects are of things experienced in my daily life. Other writings inspired by spiritual insight or current events.

My love for animals and nature, simple things that affect our lives, inspire and challenge my ability to write these poetic stories. Certain subjects are researched with an outline of historical notes. This process became as creative as the flow. It increased my knowledge and understanding of some of the simple, creative, and most beautiful things under creation.

When some of my friends ask me what I'm up to nowadays, I reply, "I'm writing poetry." They turn and snicker. After reading them a few poems, they've conveyed they like some! Or, some were a little zany and they didn't understand the story. Some reply that I should go back to what I did best, promoting concerts and events they understood.

Guess what? A lot of my poems are zany, and so am I.

Some of my poems are also deep personal thoughts and circumstances that shaped my life. These poems may comfort some readers to know they're not alone in experiencing some of these difficult, life-changing moments.

That's the fun of capturing these thoughts in poetic riddles and rhymes. I don't have to be in control, or right, or try to contract the next superstar, or sell enough tickets to pay for it. I can just dance in the rain or ride in the parade. Cast my fishing line out. Drive fifty in a fifty as passersby shout. Hug my wife. Play ninjas with my grandkid's plastic knife. Be kind to others and pray to kick out strife. Goose and deer hunt, plant in the garden, paint on a canvas, ride a horse bareback, all without leaving my chair.

That's what these poems are all about—life.

Some of the poems you may have to decipher. Listen for the joy, reflections, or zany humor. You may have to ponder the hereafter.

Blessings,
Jeffrey A Krueger

Captured

Puncturing holes with nail in the tin top
Grab glass jar fill with sticks, grass, dewdrop
Fresh air enters swirling about
Open flower with buzzing shout

Tip the cover, maneuver in
Black with yellow, fall within
Takes a few for a humming choir
Adding jumping highflyers

Mosaic wings, easy snatch
Collect from the web, delicate catch
Fuzzy crawler, ready to hatch
Mixed cocktail, will they all last?

Making friends with my mixture grew
Didn't understand or have a clue
Wasn't their home, glass-jar zoo
Screwed-off lid releasing to garden avenue

Seeing jumping green, like a gazelle
Alongside slow-moving shell
New family captured in my glass bell
Probably must let them go, as well

Feeding them small black-wing creatures
Naming Mad Max and the Preacher
How small little lives become teachers
Lasting memories first capturing procedure

Ninth in D Minor

Sand sifting through my hand
Waving colored fabric strands
Surfing twenty-foot ocean wave
Coolness of the darkened cave

Shimmering rays, sun's blinding light
Penetrating through the white
Full moon's glow
Glistening off the lake below

Beautiful images hypnotize the mind
Stomping, marching somersaults refined
Crawling, walking, running
Chasing through a passageway humming

Hands swirling, arms out, mimicking conductor's cameo
Pouring red-hot steel in the mold, refining pure gold
Joyous feeling, heart beating within
Traveling beyond time, space, celestial spin

Sundogs that sing
String sections movement, chorus of hummingbirds' wings
Butterflies fluttering magnificent kaleidoscope color
Brass calls out like a brawler

Woodwinds usher in sunrise
Calmness of the prophet who speaks wise
Conversation between glowing rainbows
Harmonious dancing, grain waving, meadows clothes

Jackhammer drilling, busting up the street
Cars' and trucks' delicate vapor released
Siren in the distance, streetcar passes by
Noon bell rings of high

Continued on next page

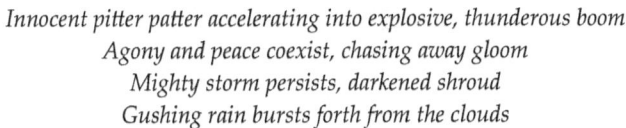

Innocent pitter patter accelerating into explosive, thunderous boom
Agony and peace coexist, chasing away gloom
Mighty storm persists, darkened shroud
Gushing rain bursts forth from the clouds

Children leaping with joy out loud
Rejoicing and celebrating the world's crowd
Weeping silence arises, to flags flowing in the wind
Reaching the finish line with a soulful grin

Victorious voices stand up, calling to all
Glorious heroes crashing through the wall
Marching to a triumphal jubilation
Revealing civilization, a visionary universal revelation

Joyful brotherhood cherubim sing
Truth flows through the score's wellspring
Divine Creator revealed in glistening stars
Completing the Father's harmonious memoirs

The Keeper

Silent moving shadow
Yaraldi, measuring first sideshow
Sun, moon, solstice, equinox
Valley of the kings' dials in a box

Second M B.C. water flow, incense
Fleeting moment past tense
Astrolabes, candles, sandglass
Reliable at sea, many amass

Pendulum sits in the swing
Harmonic oscillator that sings
Chronometer H1 to H5 tested the seas
Electric came to be, balance spring, fresh breeze

P. Henlein ornamental pendant, mainspring
Looking down to see if I am late for the King
Give me a dial, lug, case, crystal, crown, hands, bezel
Calendar chronograph unique vessel

Moon phase, tourbillon, pull of gravity
Many pieces inventive design arranged craftily
Incabloc, rotor, wheel, bridge, and barrel
Caliber, escapement, gasket, jewel, repeater, splendid apparel

Queen Vacheron Constantin Tour de I'Ile collector's dream
R. Daytona P. Newman, a scream
Address Breguet Grande, complication
Planet Graff fascination, hallucination

Mr. Citizen, D. Cartier, Mrs. Seiko, Brother Omega, Paul Casio—what a team
Sir Bulgari, Lord Piaget, Queen Longines, Prince Tissot, Captain Rado, Duke Festina—raise my esteem
Sister Patek Phillippe, Helen Chopard, Max Movado—stopped wearing in the garden
Uncle Swatch, Rocky Fossil, Professor Skagen, Mount Bulova, Colonel Timex—a bargain

Continued on next page

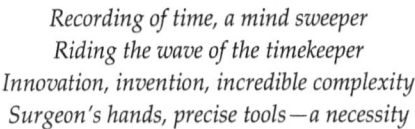

Recording of time, a mind sweeper
Riding the wave of the timekeeper
Innovation, invention, incredible complexity
Surgeon's hands, precise tools—a necessity

Our heated friend to atomic accuracy
My stomach growling rapturously
Reality of the babies' feeding time
Magical carpet ride defining abstract construct find

Grandfather stands tall in the hall
Our Father is outside the timeline of it all
Eternity of evolution says there's no end
Creation is where it all begins

Fully Known

Peeling away
Blue sky
Beneath the sunken
Surf's eyes

Typhoon shatters
Coffin's bones dry
Of the luminous
Phantom's lies

Symmetry of elegance
Nursed the disobedience
Colliding with a vision notion
Standing on the balcony

With the bleeding commotion
Gypsies' agony
Listening to the street below
Crystal tambourines in harmony

Shrouded by
Drunken silk
Scared glimpse
Of lavished sovereignty

Poor reflection
An altered beacon of soured milk
Flooding the nocturnal emptiness
Cleansing the fleshly mold with affection

Gathering up baskets
Pieces of the shattered casket
Polished fruits' glorious skin
Permeate within

Continued on next page

Changing the obituary
Purifying the banks of the estuary
Beacon of light
Born-again life to fight

Alligator Stomp

Steel jaws close down on the white
Spring-loaded keeps the nails tight
Slap, slap, slap bent pipe
Pull out the tooth with all your might

Pages of documents become close friends
Missed a few, start over again
Claw tool, release your rule
Start again to feed the mule

Would be lost without this fool
Page one missing, under my stool
Need to finish a must deadline
Have to reload but I can't find

There you are under the folders piled high
Small box stack together in line
Pry open your mouth, pull back your tongue
Load you up again, steel bullets freshly hung

Now it's time to start over, my friend
Hundreds of pieces piled high to no end
Ready for the attorney's brief at noon
Squeeze together, strong hands of a baboon

Finished in time, neatly piled high
Delivered to the courtroom just in time
My much-needed confidant chomp
Dancing together, the alligator stomp

Beacon Ukraine

Wanting to see the sunlight
Digging through rubble cement
Grabbing the bright

No war will cuff our hands
Angels have our back, now sent
So, we can stand

Home of freedom under siege, approaching near
Trying to blind our eyes so we can't see
Disaster surrounds us, launching fear

Arm in arm with comrades to roam
Stopping to crush thee
In the physical, lose our brick-and-mortar homes

In the heavenlies we're not alone
Solemn oath to lay down our lives, never flee
Saving generations' remembrance stone

Protecting humanity from nightmarish invasion plan
We may lose some of our land
We'll never give our souls to the devil's clan

Supernatural light has been loaded and released
Tanks, missiles, you may think they have the upper hand
In the heavenlies, incinerating the generational cursed beast

Innocent deaths become blood-soaked, divine ground
Burying our dead, praying God to forgive
Wrapping bodies in stained shroud

World watches with a distant applause
Shouts of peace crying out loud to live
Not realizing the enemies' insidious advance for its cause

Continued on next page

Holding freedom's banner high, we testified
Not allowing murder to be justified
Conquering with the power of the Spirit inside

Ending the bloodshed, occupation nullified
Rebuilding our country with gracious pride
Gloriously high, deep, and wide

Swirling Wind

Black in the distance
Moving fast overground
Grab my hand to outdistance
Call in the barking hound

Sirens abruptly wailing unlicensed
Lightning almost hitting the ground
Radio newscast suddenly silenced
To a roaring train sound

Huddling together in the shower tub
Covering the little ones
With a heavy mattress, curled up
Hearing pounding of bass drums

Walls shaking, vibrating
Wind howling, penetrating brick's skin
Sounds of glass smashing, breaking
Crunching walls, from a giant, swirling rolling pin

Suddenly an eerie silence begins
Stepping out with shaking hands
Nothing left but the tub, shower, faucet twins
Roof and walls all gone, standing in a wasteland

Our lives are safe, we don't know how
Thunderous, black funnel cloud took it all
We thank God for saving us, a miracle, wow
Having each other safe and sound, Lord's call

Outer Limits

Magellan set a sail
Earhart with wings
Yuri Gagarin set a trail
Aldrin, Armstrong, step on new things

Soyuz lifeboat
Skylab new habitat
Expanding border's trench coat
Curiosity top hat

Discovering dream domains
Supporting earthly life
Flexible structures, innovative gains
Outcome peaceful or a threatening knife

Robotic missions becoming clear
Fourth neighbor from the sun
Pioneering with a cheer
Recruiting drivers to have some fun

Commercial companies have opened a new gateway
Exciting new atmosphere
Old guard is passing away
Rocketing through the stratosphere

Gamma rays' eyesight
Multi wavelength eyes
Reflecting insight
Deep into heavenly skies

Oh, what a joy for the human mind to employ
Places we have yet to discover
Expanding our world to enjoy
Satisfying our scientific hunger

Saved

Light appeared to the wise
Gold, frankincense, and myrrh spiritualize
Swaddling clothes
Time has come, a planted rose

Forty-day dedication
Taught at twelve, very candid
Water flowed over, the dove landed
Forty days of temptation

Gather twelve into the kingdom
Demonstrated power revealed
Healing partnered with wisdom
Legalistic hats, truth they embezzled

Last meal together, bread of life
Foretell betrayal revealing counterfeit's lies
Washing feet, forgiveness ends the strife
Turning point, new covenant finalized

Peaceful moment with my father
Taken away without a struggle
Mock trial, denial of brothers
Pilot bets on the daily double

Flogged, thorns, purple robe
Carried his cross on his own
Nailed hands and feet, soldier's speared probe
They do not know, called up to the throne

It is finished, bowed his head
Taken away, laid in stripes of linen
Stone moved away, cloth in red
Running to tell, he has been

Continued on next page

Peace be with you
My wounds you can see
Sending you to follow through
Guided by the Holy Spirit you receive

My kingdom now perceived
Go throughout the land, shout the decree
Save from the enemies' hideous disease
Eternal life for those who believe

Precious Pebbles

As my hands sift through the rich soil
Divine privilege is given
To plant with sweat and toil
Do I have control over these boundaries?
Of many a bloody siege
Providing security, energy, and nourishment
Or will it all spoil?

Who wields the power
Of the earthly ground?
Creating a source
Of wealth and stability
Owned by the ruling elites' nobility
Kings, queens, dictators
The states' playground

Some have a home
In meadows of wheat
Sought after emotional
Ownership received
Conquering to hold and keep
So many buried in the ground
We continue to weep

Purple mountains, emerald valleys, majestic waterfalls
Beauty beyond what greed and power seeks
Creeks flowing into the river
A pathway to keep
Stewart's marching
To receive
The curtain calls

Continued on next page

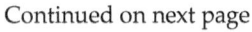

On my knees
Kissing the fertile field
Blessed are those sheltered
By the weeping willow
Souls lost in the ravine of lava's death blow
Poverties squatters
Are heavenly sealed

Riverbank of weeds
Encroaching the scenery
Violent disputes, treaties, wars, political territory
Struggle for economic assets
Immigration all transitory
Overflowing the fjord's banks and grasslands
With human slavery

Dig, drill, excavate
Clear-cutting the Amazon's plate
Human thievery
Needed for the powerful machinery
Gas, oil, gold, diamonds, lithium, coal
Can we escape?
Annihilating our wisdom, exploiting rape

Bowl of rice, a drink of clean water
Blanket for warmth
A blessed hot shower
Taking for granted our many gifts
Will humanity expose the tyrants' terrestrial tower?
Or yield to the opulent worldly myths?
Willing to be destroyed by our own selfish power

Boulders will crash
Smashing the roads into mounds of sawdust
Mountains will fall like a flash
Into the sea, entombing lust
Flames consume all that has been seen
Clay vessel will turn to dust
Eliminating garments that were bestowed in between

Continued on next page

Our precious pebbles, returning to the heavenlies
Safely flowing back to the unseen

Steel Box

Press the lever

Lower it down

Two pieces or four

Heated elements turn them brown

Marsh got the Nichrome

GE brought it along

Strite signed it on

Slots of various sizes, new program

Peanut butter, blueberry, strawberry, raspberry jam

Check the controls, it may turn to black

Can be a meal, or a crunchy-textured snack

Bacon and eggs, a side you must have

Square steel box, a loaf's grand slam

Circle Complete

Round and round I go
How to get off
I don't know
Two lanes, four lines, six lanes
Oh no! Don't stop
Go with the flow
Read the exit signs
They're moving too fast
I might crash
You're caught in the middle
I'm starting to giggle
Move to the outside
I'm getting cross-eyed
There you go
Slide off slow
That's our street
Now you're complete
Instantly experiencing roundabout feat

Little Device

Dominates my life's and my child's play
Upgrade every month
Part of my monthly pay
Spiderweb that captures
It's hard to stay away
Fits in my back pocket
Emoji lights up, I like it
Twitter de dumb, worldly prophets
Gaming away, gift-card deposit
Thumbs that move fast
Messages don't last
Do you realize I can hear you?
Standing in line
Taking over family time
Faces turn down like a mime
Stealing personal encounters and so much more
One bar, two bars, three bars, four
Controlling our thought waves
Becoming technologized slaves
Pictures and music abound
Is it worth all the frowns?
Turn on all the lights, start our car
Play a game with a new avatar
Lock the door, ticket for a plane
Yikes! Forgot my power cord, losing my brain
Can you hear me now?
Sounds like you're in a tunnel, anyhow
Am I on speaker? I hear a dog, bow wow
Zoom, I can see you, wow
Miraculous visit with the grandkids
Encyclopedia at our fingertips
Now it's on our wrist
Mini office travels afar, we won't be missed
Good things in the palm of our hand
Abuses can be instruments in this band
Lies, hate, gossip, fake stories spin

Continued on next page

Connect the daily Word for a joyful grin
Speak and share and watch good things
My provider is horrible, can't connect, there's no ring
Easy to be addicted to the fall
Remember, this little device reveals all

Beyond the Horizon

Contemplating the origin
Ethereal vision sees
Beyond the horizon
Daydream at sea
Discernable presence reveals
Existence
Of the unseen

Peeling onion of its shield
Granting tears to communicate
Scars have healed
Wounded mistakes
Surging in my soul to yield
Difficult to articulate
Time's fleeting, life's mandate

Passing through a small town
Estrange
Realizing my address's playground
Will change
Creating a mosaic
Fragments rearrange
Imparting gifts, divine exchange

Listening to the quiet
Essence of the heart
Finding opportunities
Expected, kickstart
Shining inner concentrated radiance
Bringing forth à la carte
Therapeutic fluorescence

Continued on next page

Guided by a mighty hand
Shouting hope and peace
From the grandstand
Lifting lost squire's fleece
Drowning in quicksand
Releasing unconditional love's press release
Now known to man, greatest command

Protected Bed

Spiral thread
Spiritual path just ahead
Prism structure a cord of might
Refracting angles of light

Strength reflected
Weaken from the rain injected
Soft pleasure, an intimate affair
Feeling the close, warm air

Colorful around the neck
Between the sheets, bed check
Ancient tombs of soil specs
Commodity of high respect

Eggs hatch, mulberry fed
Spinning one mile of filament, using its head
Soaked in boiling water
Unwinding a continuous thread

Remove the sericin
Biomedical sutures begin
Mighty larva contributor
World's textile, history's signature

Praise Bombyx mori, divine creature
Living on through extraction of its fiber's features
Producing delicate radiant aftermath
Immersed in a beautiful dye bath

Giving us a mosaic of colors
Satin, plain, an open weave and others
Digital or screen-print modern machine
Finishing a high lustrous sheen

Continued on next page

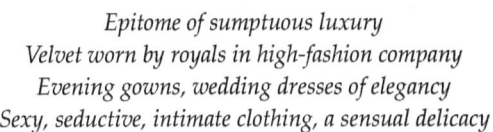

Epitome of sumptuous luxury
Velvet worn by royals in high-fashion company
Evening gowns, wedding dresses of elegancy
Sexy, seductive, intimate clothing, a sensual delicacy

Reeled from cocoons protected bed delicately

Love's Dwelling Place

What we say
   Keeps the rhythm
     What we see
       Keeps us driven
         What we believe
           Keeps the core to be forgiven
Sacrifice we must
    Patience we trust
      Center of emotion

Kindness restored
     Decency and discretion lost no more
        Love, romance, affection, an open door
      Courage to take a risk, a notion

        Compassionate hand
      Infatuation, a command

Attitude of intentions acknowledged
    Our hidden center speaks
      Flowing wisdom and knowledge
         Sustains our energy to climb the highest peaks

        Purity goes through
     Relationships renewed

Mind, will, and emotions
    Pumping blood through our veins
      Needed oxygen for the encounter to sustain

       Understanding discernment's reaction
    Conscience moral actions

Right from wrong to perceive
    Blessed are the pure for those who see

Fragile Elegance

Flawlessly amazing
Transformation
Striking alteration
Conversion by pressure
Or within

Cycle of life
Feeds on Death's bones
Completely alone
Hideously ugly afterlife
Disfigurement, reformation

Transfiguration
Renewal, heart of stone
Reflecting radiant sun's throne
Drinks nectar of might
Gleams iridescent rays of light

Blazing variation
Colorful pattern formation
Graceful, peaceful, fluttering
Transmitting rainbow's coloring
Remarkable display rediscovering

From the chrysalis cover
Emerges another
Fresh wings to travel far
Aerodynamics, clap- and- fling in the sky
Fragile elegance short-lived, goodbye

The Canvas

Hammer in the frame at night
Stretch, pull, and staple
Cover with the two-inch stick white
Place up on my wooden easel

From my brush I mix the colors on my pallet
Quenching the fire of my gentle eyes
Applying soft greens over my sketch secret
Browns mixed in among the skies

Cobalt river runs against the banks with swirling hue
Golden yellow expresses the sun's view
Casting a shaded shadow of a figure laid
Looking down on the pallet knifing baby-blue suede

Stroke of grayish black outlines an emerging cloud
Highlighted by a deep-sapphire shroud
Thin-dotted flying, lemon-eyed, white-headed proud
Emerges from the silhouette drawn within crowd

Finished off with the trees' tint of asparagus and avocado
Splash of tangelo orange and burgundy red
Autumn starts a humorous bravado
Folded in by a high-top soft-silver thread

Now I'm finished, up on the gallery wall
What home shall it befall?
Will they see beyond its colorful oil?
To find the angelic keeper of the soil

Voyage of Partaking

Ripening of a fruitful apple
Voicing bodily concerns
Weeks go by so fast
Months, a slow dance

Years slide by unintended
Sleigh of tears on every occasion
Wedding vows, babies' birth
Tragic loss, separation

Gift to see all that is realized
Overshadowing times, compromised
Blowing dandelion puffballs
Floating seeds of wishes called

Unseen heart, broken at times
War, hunger, disease
Death of mankind
Pollution of our spirit's rhyme

Divine intervention
Restoration of the soul
Forgiveness, letting go
Inner healing for the child to grow

Stories and tales of voyage's past
Of joyful times I know won't last
Kindness, legacy cast
Humble existence, a second chance

Continued on next page

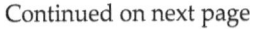

Feelings of sadness
Watching them flourish
Sometimes alone
Sense of family, the corner stone

Blessed mate
Place to escape
Sharing our life's final chapter
With love, kindness, and laughter

Silent Messenger

Curious
Countless intricate designs
Couldn't see it before
Poisoning butter
Coating my mind
By the world's clutter

Stop and smell
They say
Arrangement or bouquet
Get your hands dirty
Plant away
Peacefully relaxing, I want to stay

Pop their heads
Up from the cold
Petals and leaves
So bold
Fragrances so delicious
Blossoming seeds, uncontrolled

Parade of floats' best prize
Decorated cape
Wedding crown of grace, romanticize
In my sickness brings moment of escape
Delicately wrapped, Mother's surprise

This one, unpopular in the neighborhood
Familiar to the world, unique specimen
Golden blooms, lions' tooth leaves stood
Once an abundance of food and medicine
Magical yellow, friends' childhood

Continued on next page

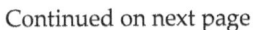

So many colors, shapes, categories
Divine masterpiece, vibrant relation
Expressing visual stories
Countless celebrations
Unspoken words, Valentine's glory
Expressing joy, love, romance, congratulations

Oh, That's a Big One

Dip the wand
In soapy sugar water
Blow gently, watch it wander

Bigger circle submerged after
Creating large, moving oval splendor
Floating by with laughter

Little ones, so amazed
A joyous performance
Capturing their gaze

Cost is very little
Watching see-through spheres float away
From this amazing tittle

Of jubilant children's play

Fenced Patch

Nailing wooden planks one by one
Could be a lot of fun
Splashing on whitewash in knickers
Easing my workday jitters

Keeping out the critters
Adding some bitters
From the greens planted, I think
Breaking for a refreshing drink

Running by a bandit, fluffy white
Staying out of sight
Loves those carrots, radishes too
Hiding with his buddy raccoon

Russian sage, yarrow, and lavender
Leaving the gate open, not clicking the fastener
Keeping those varmints at bay
Adding scarecrow keeps birds away

Luscious red tomatoes, lunchtime snack
Fitting in my travel backpack
Onions, lettuce, cucumber snackers
Eating sweet peas like tasty crackers

Peppers, sweet, spicy, and hot
Adding spinach to the lot
Garlic added taste, squash with butter
Loving my growing spot, as I cutter

Close friends Mr. and Mrs. Herbs, cheerfully
Rosemary, basil, parsley
Adoring famous comrades
Feeding the hungry families' nomads

34

Shared Life

Bonding with the steam
Bowl of mixed greens
A freshly baked potato, sour cream
Sharing fun-filled dreams

Communicating openly
Eating tasteful morsels ceremoniously
Fragrance of stirred fried vegetables
Invading our conversation parables

Stories told bringing laughter
Tears of sadness of our friends' disasters
Trusting together as we gather
Breaking of sourdough bread, butter matters

Sliced thin by the chef's hand
Roasted turkey, steak, with ham
Sipping of wine, cleansing the palate
Celebrating together, thankful salad

Tastebuds ready for a sweet desire
Cream-filled chocolate cake, pacifier
Listening intently, teaching hour
Opinions about the world's power

Belonging, secure, safe from the daily quake
Pouring the dark brew to stay awake
Community of one, two, three, our family
Recipe for friendships together blissfully

Clinking of glasses, a toast
Happy, gratitude, ultimate host
Consumed fulfillment, no loss of weight
To the glorious empty plate

Lost and Found

Gather, gather, gather
Buy, buy, buy
Million-dollar homes, gate crasher

Straw shack

Stacks upon stacks
So many things acquired
Rubies, diamonds, gold, avoid tax

Bathroom in a hole

One car, two cars, garage full
How much stuff can I own?
Jet airplane, one time zone to the next, roomful

Mules must rest

Ageing rust has started to collect
Bathing in my treasures
Losing my breath, a disconnect

Praying for fresh rainwater

Blinded by my lust
My worldly possessions
Are turning to dust

I'm hungry, bread found

My skin wrinkles like worn-out covers
Understanding the most important purchase
Love and care for others

Continued on next page

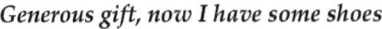

Generous gift, now I have some shoes

No longer seek the material coffins
My soul's renewed, a new playground
Gathering heaven's treasures softened

You were lost, but now you're found

What You Say?

Gibal Jaabal
Good climb

Nafiy Somaki
Space defined

Nooper Lacooper
Rocks to find

Prizzle Duphy
Conquer time

Wribbles Quabble
Get behind

Schmeic Haim
Drooling slime

Fungy Staly
Not a crime

Mugget Fugel
Little grime

Wigget Legy
About a mime

Lasneaky Ssnack
Eat Key lime

Tutto Godall
Silly rhyme

One Tine, Two Tines, Three Tines, Four

Bronze Age Qijia culture, the first
Bones from Gansu view
Cause God-fearing skepticism, an outburst
Theophanu added to the debut

Latin Furca too large for the mouth
One tine, two tines, three tines, four
No use when there's a drought
Marriage of silver, shrunken foot of a dinosaur

Two sticks lost the war
Homeless, starving bowl won
Scooping cousin couldn't stab the boar
Thanksgiving meal, needed for everyone

Sheltered safely in the kitchen drawer
Used as a weapon when an intruder steps in
Much rather use it to pry open the trap door
Comrade to help slice steak so thin

Slides off my plate, I can't win
Which one do I use on the table of the queen?
Trade in the antique silver with a grin
Assisting friend included in our life routine

First Summer Ride

Off the porch
Tip upside down
Oil the chain
Ready to ride uptown

Wash it up
Adjust the brakes
Check the gears
Safety light no mistake

Helmet on
My first pedal
Going around the lake
Push down hard on the metal

Pleasant rush of wind
Caresses my skin
Green passes like a shark's fin
Blue has a majestic grin

Freedom like wings of eagle
Coasting down the hill
Car pulls out illegal
Almost take a spill

Imagination, racecar alive
Spin around the corner
Off cozy sunny drive
Gliding into Main Street like a foreigner

Chain it up to pillar stone
Licking ice-cream cone
Find my way back home
Summer ride refreshing cologne

Again, Again, Again

Crying out in anguish
Horrific gut-wrenching pain
How to stop the insane

Agony of senseless violence
No answers to this madness rain
Unwanted affliction so poisonous

Fabric of kindness torn
Compassion traded for scorn
Minds damaged by an evil norm

Moral compass broken
Support structures shattered, disconnected
Infested cancer, minds spoken

Solutions must endeavor
Walls, locks, protector, laws, presented
Freedoms lost forever

Grief beyond measure
Hearts broken and tormented
Heavenly reunion, our hope's treasure

Pray to reveal the trespassers
Faith must prevail represented
Casting down violent emperors

Halting again, again, again the demented

See Through

Test tube of ingredients
Poured into the flask
Falling from obedience
Creating a glazed mask

Cathedrals of shaped colors
Forming a vitrum porcelain cover
Hidden by dollars
Worshiping the mother

Skylines of stainless-steel fittings
Erecting reflective bulletproof maze
Finding bones in the diggings
Revealing ancient essays

Begging for mercy
Transparency cuts its way
Casting out all controversy
Seen through the protective rays

Panels open to the fresh air
Closed to the stormy haze
Insulating shattered, broken affair
Cuts deeply into the fleshly praise

Maze of optical fibers
Now severed from the soul
Refraction of the light upon the bribers
Exposes the keyhole

Turn the key to open
Solarium of hope and joy
Find it on divine doorstep spoken
Seeing through the brokenness of the healed boy

Tonbo

Many names they call
Beginning of summer for all
Its amazing sign
Thousands flying iridescent shine

Gentle and fragile helicoptering in
Propel six directions with a grin
Aerial ambush to eat their prey
Compound eyes see 360 ways

Rebirth of happiness, ancient folklore
Millions of years before the dinosaur
From the sleepy cold
Eating skeeters by the load

Simulating a gentle breeze
Living underwater before the siege
Barometers of wetland's health
Few weeks losing their colorful wealth

I'll miss those masters of the air
Landing on my arm to declare
Charming my gazing stare
Return again, beginning the summer flare

Everlasting

She lost her hair
Ring the bell, a tremendous day
Nurses took care

Family meal strengthens the hive
Holding hands to pray
Newborn baby to arrive

Playing in the sandbox space
Tender moments watching them grow
Encouragement to win the race

Compassion to care
Respect for life, bestow
Tears to share

Colorful flowers sing
Peace the gift of winter cold
Refreshing birth of spring

Friendships to embrace
Gathering together, behold
On a quilted blanket of grace

Overcoming the obstacle
Joyous sobbing within
The essence so powerful

Don't hide our love
In the loneliness trails of a hateful grin
Descends the peaceful dove

Hug the earth's human core
Miracle feelings, hard to express
Always believing for much, much more

The Greatest, the Most Important

Intimate affection
All day conversation, a transformer
Your welcome direction

Bathe in the water
Guide to the street corner
Wear new clothes to escape the slaughter

Attend to their needs
Encounter all joyfully
Pull out the deceptive weeds

Care for the sick
As precious royalty
Directed by the lighted candlestick

Encourage my brother and sister
Keep their eyes on the prize
Compassion and grace a nurturing listener

Intercede against weariness
Fight for the crown to be spiritualized
Grow in faith and forgiveness

Escape the road of self-doubt
Listen to the angel's shout
The most powerful kingdom route

Love God and love people
That's what it's all about
Proclaim it from the steeple

My Favorite Space

Four corners' hours of play
Dig, dig, dig steam shovel
Pail makes a castle-top display

Dozer creates a road
Blast a tunnel
Mountain hole, hops a toad

Water pours into the moat
Making brown pies
Dinosaurs jump into the boat

Soldiers protect the wall
Helicopter lands from the sky
Building stick bridge over the waterfall

Discarded cups, pots, and pans
Builders' tools
Form a face with my hands

Hours of building, shaping
Citadel complete with seashell jewels
Turtle warriors escaping

Squishy cold between the toes
Approaching baby brother, destructive cyclone
Mud balls he throws

Stop, stop! You're crushing the pirate's home
Momentary minute, the king lost his throne
Darn, I wanted to crush and stomp that castle dome

I think I'd rather play in my box alone

Illusions

Tiptoe on a rainbow
Periscope in my mason jar
Cookies without dough
Catch the star
Coat of trash
Celestial trolley car
Drinks of volcanic ash
Raindrops of time's reservoir
Fossil of an eyelash
Ventriloquist costar
Lizards with masks
Gravity's radar
Drink the sun's flask
Clouds with faces
Turtles' sea king
Costumes in cases
Oceans that sing
Elevator to moon bases
Invisible being's shoestring
Portal to Mars races
Trees that dance worshiping
Twenty-lane highways to workplaces
Cars that fly air spring
Robots that share
Dreams with deaf ears
Subway's childcare
Smoke with cheers
Legless chair
Cloak with mirrors
Eagle's stare
Cards that disappear
Curve-ball affair
Language of Shakespeare
Humans that care

Color Crayons

Many shades from far away
Came to stay
True display

Variety like no other
Inspiring one another
So many suffered

Innovation released
Competition's feast
Woven threads increased

Cord cannot be broken
Silent voice has spoken
Living in the land of the chosen

One-of-a-kind palette
Crayons of every color talent
What flag to fly to inhabit

Boat of freedom
Sails of truth, we need some
Embracing the gift, beating the drum

Parting the veil
From the hidden face of fear's devastating trail
Come together to persevere and prevail

Expose the lies
Color in the shadow lines of disguise
Experiment continues, will we destroy the prize

Continued on next page

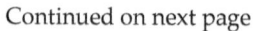

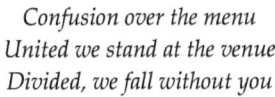

Confusion over the menu
United we stand at the venue
Divided, we fall without you

Greatest melting pot
Have their voices forgot?
Peace and freedom they sought

Amazing Sticks

Open the shade, 120 suns' colorful rays
Stay within the lines, they say
Playful tools for a rainy day
Available at the exclusive restaurant on the bay

Jumbo, washable, triangular, skin tones, purple mountain majesty
Bright and brilliant, including macaroni and cheese
On my toast is jazzberry jam, two more please
Razzmatazz, a pink flamingo prances in the breeze

Peel back the paper to see
Page after page of scribbling a shade tree
Imagination set free
From a waxy material — who would believe?

Encaustic painting, then Lemercier and Franklin
Alice coined the name in 1903 and banks in
Featured yellow box in postage-stamp wins
Barney and Smith receive the gold medal with a grin

Oh, what joy these boxes of presents give
Millions of children's drawings, adults relive
Thankful for the invention that gives
Crayola a hundred years, outlives

Once Upon a Breakfast

Same cards they drew
Who knew music would be the glue?

Veteran dealmaker, visionary seeker
Self-feeder, spiritual sweeper

Arrogant counselor, angry moments
Mixed together, rainbow components

Walking narrow paths of disparity
Building bridges of parity

Years of erecting a fort
Successful worldly passport

Disagreements embraced
Partnership erased

Embedded caring hearts display
Sicknesses and bodies start to decay

Praying for healing perceived
Kids and grandkids, gifts received

Sharing the journey achieved
Brotherly friendship conceived

Veggie omelet, please
Two eggs sunny, bacon and cheese

My Son

Gift of birth
No gold to match your worth
Playtime fun
Sharing with everyone

Young boy
Schooltime joy
Watching you grow
Running in the meadow

Now a man ablaze
Choose your ways
How tall you stand
Reaching out with a guiding hand

I cared for you so many days
Hoping you would escape the maze
Praying always
Giving my Heavenly Father praise

God has spoken no more delays
My pain will last until those days
I see you again in the divine rays
We'll talk again, as always

My faith stands through this crushing blow
In my sadness and grief, God will show
Guiding path, He won't let me go
For my son is with him, this I know

Colors Light the Sky

Loud explosion everywhere
My wiener dog gets so scared
China started this ruckus
Celebrations all about us

Noise, light, smoke, a confetti missile
Bang, crackle, hum, and whistle
Bend my head back, I get a crink
Smell the gunpowder stink

Red strontium, white aluminum
Orange calcium, yellow sodium
Green barium, violet potassium
Music matched, directed from the podium

Amazing shapes and sizes
Fill the evening sky with colorful surprises
Palm tree, peony spherical ring reflects a heart
Roman candle crisscrossing, spider bursts apart

Trailing stars, a timed rain
Weeping willow as we sip champagne
New Years we salute with a flash and a bang
Independence shared with the family gang

Kids love the sparklers and fun
Festivities of memories spun
Of nonviolent times when we got along
Thunderous spectacle of a combustible gong

Illuminating our human dignity
Experiencing a lightshow symphony
Shining brightly on symbolic occasions
Less than a few hours, continuing hundreds of generations

Continued on next page

Sky embraces this passionate moment
Joyous smiles, oohs and aahs, a reactive component
Muffed ears of sleeping little ones
Quiet now, colors that light the sky are done

Defending the Fort

Inner eye learning
First sun in the morning
Achievements we greet
Last light before night's sheet
Fifteen stars and fifteen stripes
Dangerous struggle against bagpipes

View from the wall, a grand bright ray
New missiles exploding in the sky's highway
Testimony to the lone cloth's remaining skin!
Shout out magnificent symbol that wins
Covering the ground for freedom
Residence of courageous deed done

Sang at millions of sporting events
One hundred years after its contents
Embraced by eighteen presidents
Patriotic defense
Unity that ties and binds us together
Ultimate family marriage feather

Reflecting our historic resolve
Conquering the enemies' attempt to dissolve
Gifts of liberty with its cost
Allegiance and loyalty to righteousness sought
In God we trust
Sign of victory shall wave, it must

Lifted Up

Walking through the garden's altars
Roses with no thorns extreme
Sipping the cool waters
Of the peaceful current's stream
Approaching elk walkers
Magnificent horns supreme
Captured in a momentary
Sleepy daydream

Lily pads float so softly
Companion at my side
Pants faithfully
Trees stand tall provide
Shaded canopy
Sun's rays dancing through
The tangle gracefully

Oh, how I long
Hearing the birds' song
Restful glide
Of the eagles' flight
Releasing thoughts inside
From the earth's wrongs' bite
Staring up at stars wide
At midnight

Time to heal
Being refilled
Joyous comforts seal
Of the deep silence still
Glorious color wheel
Listening to the hummingbirds
Drinking from the cup
Of soft encouraging words

Instantly lifted up

Cause and Effect

Freedom

Follows the rule of law

Conceiving stability

Rule of law is guided by the paw

Of our capability

Justice, righteousness we draw

Highlighting our dignity

Honesty, morality foresaw

Engraving of compassion killing bigotry

Kindness and love, powerful jaw

Of divine wisdom willfully

Presiding over contentment's bed of straw

Producing joy and peace vividly

Dangerous Play

Fearful myths of the warrior's moves
Through the hidden shadowy blue
450 million years ago proves
Solitary hunter of the deep I roam to

Predator I am
Thousands of teeth array
Magnetic field, my hunting telegram
Smelling to see when striking my prey

Rolling eyes backward
At my delightful feeding
Vomit ejecting the unwanted herbs
Scent of the currents, of their bleeding

Risen to the surface, I come so slow
I wave my arm for all to see
Fifteen of my cousins you know
Greenland an oldie on the marquee

Rumors of my poisonous flesh
Shapeshifting at command
Spiritual connection, I attest
Circle of protection for my clan

My reputation has been soiled
Megalodon might have eaten you
You don't taste good, I'm spoiled
Dolphins, seals, tasty morsels I pursue

A snack I would like
So don't wiggle your legs or your hands
I might make a mistake and strike
But I'd rather be friends if we can

Days Before Today

Tomorrow's decision
Miracle collision

Compass is broke
Smothered with black cloak

Losing my bearing
Clouds staring

Out of control sleigh
Molding of the clay

Divine intervention
Change the direction

Kids are grown up
Morning coffee cup

Memories that I share
Relaxing in my armchair

Thankful for my blessings
Colorful window dressings

History with its laughs
Walking down many paths

Tears of joy cast
Heartfelt moments in the past

Like a blanket for warmth
Love came forth

Granting a peaceful way
Embracing days before today

Divine Gift

Cultivated from seed
The world it feeds
445 million acres
Supplying all the bakers

9600 BC first cultivated
Southeastern Turkey located
Mount Karaca Dag
Emmer filled the shoulder bag

Carbohydrates, vegetable, protein
Processed in a food machine
Adhesive properties
Consumers favored these

Plowed and harrowed
Seed drill takes the highroad
Furrows bygone
Crop rotation, carry on

Horse-drawn tractor pulled along
Reaping, thrashing, gathering, winnowing song
Kernel, beard, stem, flag leaf
Reaper binder gone, combine clan is now the chief

Twenty varieties, seven species, genetic engineering
Riding in the machine with GPS steering
Beware, eyespot, blotch, strip rust, powdery mildew
Gang of four make the job easy to do

Hard spring, hard winter, soft white
Noodles, pies, pastries, cakes, cookies, take a bite
Bread, porridge, crackers, biscuits, pancakes
Pizza, muffins, rolls, vodka, put on the brakes

Continued on next page

Beautiful, tiny grain
Sustaining life's reign
When combined has mighty power
Divine gift to grow the human flower

Every Breath

From the womb
Childhood summer play
Brother and sister's way
Fireworks that boom

Friends that stayed
Crayfish, dragonflies, frogs
Creek with mossy bogs
Forest walk parade

Granny's home, sheltered the firestorm
Appreciation for the move
Available to sleep, cold empty back room
New schools, transform

Parents pain, reflected lost virtue
Comforting others, discernment
Gift navigating internal darkness, in earnest
Holy Spirit's better view

Spring's sun melting snow
Ocean waves respectfully lapping
Warm rain graciously clapping
Flowers blossoming glow

Traveling to far-off places
Grateful to my soulmate's connection
Children's energy injection
Health for running the bases

Dogs that lick our face
Moon's rays shimmer on night lake
Sunsets, make no mistake
New baby to embrace

Continued on next page

Hummingbirds playing the kazoo
Bears, elephants, hippos, kangaroos
All the animals in the zoo
Take time to taste the stew

Snowflake's symmetry
Bees making honey
Clouds that look funny
Humankind's creative imagery

God's vision for all to see

Unspoken Language

Romantic kiss, tenderness
One flesh affection, effortless
Nursing breast, gentleness
First bath, closeness

Kindergarten bus, separation anxiety
Birthday celebration, kindhearted gaiety
Christmas gifts, thoughtful variety
Admired talent and notoriety

Release of the two-wheeler suspension
Instruction on driving the motorized invention
Graduations, diplomas, new direction
Promise Keepers convention

Surgery, caring, recovery
Revealing addiction, compassion's symphony
Sharing wounds, thoughtful discovery
New being so lovely

Prayers of reconciliation
New home, construction anticipation
Pet's final sleep, painful narration
Reflecting on life's creation

Embrace from a friend
Hug mother and father, welcomed dividend
Tears for our lost loved one's end
Memories transcend

Nature's reflection
Faith in the resurrection
Divine connection
God's intimate, everlasting affection

Soft Splendor

Second century BC
Yan Zhitul year 531, revealing quote
Ten million packages, Ming Dynasty
Added perfume, spoke

When the squares weren't
Water, rags, sand, leaves, seaweed, corncob
Sometimes a river current
Necessary cleaning job

Strip the bark, and chipped
Digestion of the pressure cooker
Fibers cleaned, bleached, and dipped
Water sprayed, screen onlooker

Scraped and wound on reels
Cut the strip and perforate
Rolls, rolls, rolls to peel
In the dispenser rotated

Struggle in public enclosure
Backwards to low
Tearing to pieces finger exposure
The box is empty, oh no!

Safe at home at last
Pulls out easy on my lap
Several folds, strength that pass
Softer two ply, no chap

Almost lost my trusted friend
A pandemic hoarding trend
Might have pulled a page from magazine's end
Comfortable on my porcelain throne, I descend

Double-Edge Sword

Articulating understanding
Hurtful stabbing, crash landing
Foulness with no meaning
Encouraging, gentle, fruitful conveying

Open the stable doors, no return pronouncing
Pulling the reins back from trouncing
Life-giving or decay, can I command?
Calling out a powerful army on demand

Flickering light is illuminating
Parched thirst in translating
Fanning the spark or denouncing
Stopping the treacheries from announcing

Life or death imposed
Which journey have I chose?
Casting out the line of deadly poison
Restraint has moistened

Tear it down, build it up
Hatred or love fill the cup
Tame the muscle conductor
Arrogance or jealous instructor

Guard with a muzzle
Place light pieces in the puzzle
Guide with a small rutter
Smooth rough edges by inner stonecutter

Inked Quill

Composing a song, searching out a love gone
Combination of such things is intriguing to me, I'm drawn
Creating a mark, a form, symbols that shape it
Leaves of passages, traveling roads, tale of wit
Shakespeare virtuoso with ingenious flair
Etched the page with diverse affair

Constructing imagination, multi lanes empower
Ambition, success, then failure, wilted flower
Plank after plank fashion the footbridge
Crossing over to sunlit meadow's ridge
Planting seed after seed, viewing magical bounty
Lengthy journey on the horse-ridden Mountie

Exquisite art, beauty by nature's expression
Civil liberties, antislavery was the confession
Relationships found in profound realism's victory
Evolution deep theory, afterlife's mystery
Heal illiterate poor children, lessons of history
Blossoms of voices, revealed swiftly

Erie night darkness, chilling horror, allusions
Racism battles, searching nostalgic conclusions
Flamboyant diamond cutter revealing the macabre
Rejection, totalitarianism swinging from the candelabra
Adventurous fables, eyes of the watchmakers, precise tools of peace
Jealousy, chivalry, capturing winds of fantasy's golden fleece

Childhood memories, battle between dark and light
Raw emotions, investigator's retrieval, satisfied appetite
Time-travel voyageurs
Self-indulgence becomes a fairytale in years
Yankee spirit proclaimed, masked humor
Children's answer, comic parables embedded tumor

Continued on next page

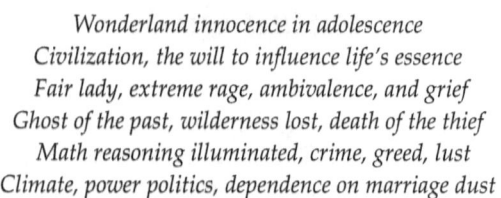

Wonderland innocence in adolescence
Civilization, the will to influence life's essence
Fair lady, extreme rage, ambivalence, and grief
Ghost of the past, wilderness lost, death of the thief
Math reasoning illuminated, crime, greed, lust
Climate, power politics, dependence on marriage dust

Wizards' death train, searching folktales
Protest of education, God's details
Super science, dystopian future
Piloting fourth dimension, stitched suture
Pieces of skilled deliverers of thought
Assembled in the basket of fruit that sought

Cooking these tasty morsels in sauce
Manifest all things not lost
Clothed together hat, shirt, pants, and shoes
Full deck of cards, aces I choose
Courier delivers the expressive mail
Brightens my day with words that avail

Majestic Adventure

History past, a cruel dance
Disturbing circumstance
So young to wear the diamond weight
Pledge defender of the faith to advocate

Romantic love, so endearing
Darkest shadows persevering
Revealing stability
During hostility

Affection for horses, country estate
Corgis were first, no mistake
Children, grandchildren, picnics abound
Serving guests without servers of the crown

Falling bombs on humanity
Rising above all the insanity
Voice of wisdom to the Bulldog
Thirteen more, warm affectionate dialogue

Suez affair with great support
Conversation around subject's report
Brief interlude from the strikes
Headmistress lecturing the comforting mother, yikes

Scandalous estrangement, divorce
Death of People's Princess, charities force
Outpouring affection, dereliction to provide an olive leaf
Publicly joined the grief

Imitating Scottish accent, Iraq War
Financial independence, fifth cousin adored
Brexit process, time derailed
Sympathetic voice prevailed

Continued on next page

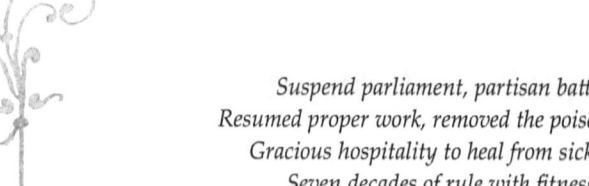

Suspend parliament, partisan battle
Resumed proper work, removed the poison apple
Gracious hospitality to heal from sickness
Seven decades of rule with fitness

Grace, dignity, dedication—the world's treasure
Traveling the globe with supreme measure
Rock of stability, continuity, history's emissary
Elegance, style, deep family love, extraordinary

Procession winding down the country streets
Viewed by the world, a solemn sleep
Regal march laid at rest at the palace complex
Adoring thousands paying their respects

Ninety-six bells ring out to tell
Astonishing life, finishing the race well
Testimony, family, faith, service, a dove
"Grief is the price we pay for love"

Beautiful Bean

Sufi monasteries, in Persia wed
Santa Domingo, Brazilian led
Ocean journey, seeds spread
Purple fruit joined with red

Picking, drying, hulled, depulping
Raw green, roasted chestnut, brown resulting
Savor, flavors, complex aromatic exulting
First crack, second crack, now consulting

Steam rising from this rich black
Aroma consumes the nasal track
First rising, brightness unpacked
Pleasurable moment, energized attack

Warmth on the hands as I sip
Soothing, relaxing courtship
Engage my senses in fellowship
Easing off the landing strip

One pour, two pours, never through
Up all night, joyous dark brew
Consuming jester, passing through
Awaken gift for your sense's euphoric avenue

My Companion

Waiting in the field of green
Ever alert with pointed ears so keen
Steady movement to nature's changer
Aware of ever-present danger

Rearing back, eyes ablaze
Divine wings, outstretched praise
Tremendous, thundering dash
Distant from the world's clash

Gliding through the misty dew
Iron muscles stretched so firm, stirring a dusty hue
Of the morning bright
Claiming forceful winds of elegance and might

Sudden stop
Causing momentary whiplash
Peaceful moment, head dropped
Forage within the grass

Hoofs pumping blood to the heart
Sixth sense, unique perception, impart
Sensitive emotions
Sounds of the surrounding ocean

Fear, joy, anger, gust-filled anxiety
Gentle loyalty, passionate gaiety
Reading reflective mirror of the soul
Spiritual bond, extol

Cradling the back with my frame
Forming a deep loving bond, we claim
Around the neck, gentle hanging arms
Experiencing a magical, tranquil charm

Continued on next page

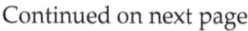

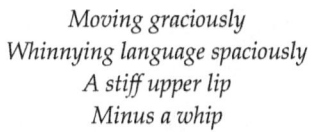

Moving graciously
Whinnying language spaciously
A stiff upper lip
Minus a whip

No incumber or bit
Loving farewell, freedom admit
Slap behind my sweet pet
Riding off into a sunset

Magnetic North

Plummeted from the high mountain peak
Losing the way through the forest deep
Backpack of tools lost
Cutting a path to cross
Honesty, purity, integrity, compass' broken glass
Lead to the stream's pass
Stumbling over river rocks
Taking a drink from wisdom's box
Stabilized by the walking stick
Clarity through the thick
Hindered by a stone wall, covered in moss
Cunning, wicked wolf's teeth, dripping sauce
Tyrant of turmoil, breath of insidious evil
Decaying body, vulture feeds gleeful
Violence, slavery, abuse, torture, tasty morsels fly
Immorality becomes morality as clouds pass by
Claws of desensitizing penetrate innocent skins
Diabolical annihilation of kindness begins
Sun's rays blocked by the veil, distorted lies to see
Dehumanizing acts, burning down the trees
Violence, murder, rape, sexual predation
Proof, accuser to the accused, applauded narration
Carelessness, recklessness, thoughtless despair
Tourniquet stops profuse bleeding, narcissist's affair
A splint to hike through the thorny gossip entanglement
Reaching the clearing, hope's fulfillment
Pick the fruits of rejuvenation, renewal, relationships
Rediscover our compassionate solutions
Dismantle damaging illusions
Standing solid ground, cherish the inspiration of forgiveness
Rest in the field of joy, peace, patience, Christmas
Magnetic North will never leave our existence

Delightful Bite

Juicy taste as I sip
Quenches my wanting parched lips

Picked to shed the green clothes
Hold ripened golden peel, pose

Expose rose-pink blush
Intense sweetness with a rush

Pollen captures the color adorned
Of fertile segments no longer scorned

Beautiful scent, fragrance escapes
Coat of tough texture, to penetrate

Mix of sweet and sour, delicious flavor
Fuzzy skin, titillating succulent savor

Flesh of white or yellow, joyous glow
Oval, purple, red, smooth, tasteful combo

Thick tannic skin, bitter, sharp
Tamed by the gentle harp

Exciting anticipation to meet again
Apple, orange, peach, and grape, delicious friends

Listen to the Light

Listen to the light shining through my window
Listen to the light shine through me

Listen to the light shining through my window
Listen to the light shine through me

And you know that it's love
Don't cry because
All the ways that you go
Can't you see it's a show

Listen to the light shining through my window
Listen to light shine through me

Listen to the light shine through my window
Listen to the light shine through me

Shine through meeeeeeeeeeeee

Silly, Silly World

Walking slowly to the park
Going to give my life a new start
No money in my pocket
No claim to fame
In this world's silly, silly game

Looking past my broken heart
Still feeling that missing part
Can you feel the pain?
I won't stay the same
In this world's silly, silly game

Battle for my life
Chance to make it right
No time to hesitate
I won't stay the same
In this world's silly, silly game

I look up to the sky
Clouds always tell me why
A little about my name
I won't stay the same
In this world's silly, silly game

In this world's silly, silly game
In this world's silly, silly game

Take a Chance

Has anyone heard about the day
When the sun refused to shine?
Will it be dark
Or will it be cold?
Where no love will ever go

When you hear this song
Your heart will light up
It won't be long
Don't be fooled by all the tears
We live in this world without any fears

Realize
Take a chance
On a new rock 'n' roll dance
Energy
Picks you up
Turns you around, now strut your stuff

Take a chance
On a newwww dance
It will lead
To another romance

Behind the mask of the eyes
Lies a dancer in disguise
They're never going to stop till the sunrise

Take a chance
On a newwwww dance

Are you tired now?
Have you had enough?
I like to dance with you
Can we shake it up?

Continued on next page

Realize
Take a chance
On a new rock 'n' roll dance
Energy
Picks you up
Turns you around now, strut your stuff

Take a chance
On a newwww dance
It will lead
To another romance

American Pilots

American pilots
Our flesh has been torn
American pilots
Whose soul is deformed
American pilots
Burning off my rust
American pilots
I can't be crushed

American pilots
Restoring my worth
American pilots
Returning to earth
American pilots
Flying on the wings of a dove
American pilots
Spreading love

American pilots
Our future is at stake
American pilots
Repair the mistakes
American pilots
Change course before it's too late
American pilots
Stop the hhhhhhate!

American pilots hey, hey, hey
American pilots hey, hey, hey
American pilots hey, hey, hey
American pilots hey, hey, hey

It's OK

Don't be so cold
Earth can't be sold
No silence, we shout
Life will come about

Yeah, it's OK
Yeah, it's OK
Yeah, we do care

I move my legs
Turn my head
Open my eyes
Hope's not dead

Yeah, it's OK
Yeah, it's OK
Yeah, we do care

We join our hands
Stomp our feet
Unite this land
To a steady heartbeat

Yeah, it's OK
Yeah, it's OK
Yeah, we do care

We struggle for peace
Against the sea
From tyrannical beast
For a world to be free

Continued on next page

Yeah, it's OK
Yeah, it's OK
Yeah, we do care

Radio soldiers
Hear our voice
Time is now
To make a choice

Yeah, it's OK
Yeah, it's OK
Yeah, we do care

Love-Tough Day

Now you know it's a love-tough day
Now you know it's a rough-tough way
Please don't blow your mind away
Cause you know we'll help you find your way

Will help you find your way
Back home
You don't have to be alone
Come with us, be with me
Because you know
You've got to believe

Now you know it's a love-tough day
Now you know it's a rough-tough way
Please don't blow your mind away
Cause you know we'll help you find your way

I've been waiting a long, long time
If you can't hold on
We will find time
Reach out
Seek out new friends
We can share love
Again, and again

Now you know it's a love-tough day
Now you know it's a rough-tough way
Please don't blow your mind away
Cause you know we'll help you find your way

Earth to Love

Earth to love
Earth to love
Earth to love
Where are you?

I am a native of this land
My father's bones are in the sand
You asked me if I am aware
Of life waiting out there

Love to earth
Love to earth
Love to earth
Where are you?

Feel the sunshine
Touch the sky
Ask the ocean
To wash blindness from your eyes

Earth to love
Earth to love
Earth to love
Where are you?

Missing my deep feelings
I once thought I had
Now I am surrounded
By the world's endless fade

Love to earth
Love to earth
Love to earth
Where are you?

Continued on next page

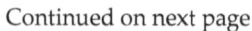

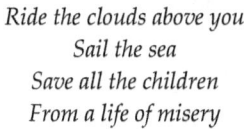

Ride the clouds above you
Sail the sea
Save all the children
From a life of misery

Earth to love, love to earth
Earth to love, love to earth
Earth to love, love to earth

It's a Wish

Some people in the city
Try to make it rich
I've got the country
Isn't life a wish?

It's a wish
It's a wish
It's a wish
It's a wish of mine

You do what you want to
You don't always know why
If you come a little closer
I'll tell you no lies

It's a wish
It's a wish
It's a wish
It's a wish of mine

We're murdering our children
Each and every day
You asked me what to do now
I just bow my head and pray

It's a wish
It's a wish
It's a wish
It's a wish of mine

We're polluting our water
Destroying our land
Puncturing our hearts
We've got to take a stand

Continued on next page

It's a wish
It's a wish
It's a wish
It's a wish of mine

Magical Lady

Broke away from my TV set
Took a stroll downtown
Having so much fun

Slipped into the local dancehall
Trying to find her
There she was

Magical lady, where were you?
Gone from my life

Danced all night
We fell in love
Ask her for a date

She said to me
It's time to leave
But it's just begun

Magical lady, where were you?
Gone from my life

Driving fast on the county road
Moonshine shines bright
She is so cold

Park my car
On her daddy's lawn
Said to me, "You can't stay long"

Gave her a kiss and a
Hug for the night
Can't you see I'll be all right?

Continued on next page

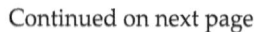

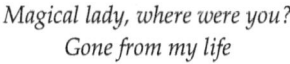

Magical lady, where were you?
Gone from my life

Very next day, jumped out of bed
Call my love
She was dead

Cried all day
Cried all night
Never thought I'd be all right

Magical lady, where were you?
Gone from my life

Burning flames
Have taken my love
Someday I'll meet her up above

Mending my broken heart
I will remember when
We had so much fun

Magical lady, where were you?
Gone from my life

Slow Moving

Knock, knock, are you there?
Under that bone there's no hair
Swim so slowly, all alone
Quiet elegance, colorful stone

Defensive shield, mighty armor
Endurance, strength, longevity, charmer
Aquarium painted friends to bond
Pool branches and leaves to climb on

Catch your breath and down you go
Freshwater and oceans show
Up on the beach to lay eggs
Digging holes with front legs

Living across the globe
Retract sideway or backward under the robe
Threatened by the extension of their homes
Will the ninjas protect with KC Jones?

What's Its Name?

Swirling above the ocean floor
Disturbance formed before
Mixing stew of warm water and wind
Hungry appetite begins

Soon it will be named
May have to cancel the baseball game
Moving slowly over the Atlantic basin
Reinforce the wall, call the brick mason

Warnings have been sent, evacuations
Store shelves picked bare, anticipation
Boarding up windows, batten down the hatches
Generator, gas, food, water, candles, and matches

Slamming into coastal towns, force of an iron sledge
Giant bulldozer of wind pushes water over the edge
Life-threatening catastrophic flooding
Roofs tore off, trees uprooted, flying debris, ducking

Howling wind increases, increases, increases
Trees bow to the ground, snap to pieces
Homes crumble, hanging on for dear life
Eye passes calm blue sky, silence before extreme strife

Wall of force returns, devouring its victims in its path
Shutting down power, fearful darkness' wrath
Minutes seem like hours in this surrounding nightmare
Hope and pray for our life to be spared

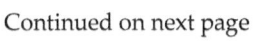

Continued on next page

Sitting on the roof, waiting to be rescued
Three children, bottle of water, loaf of bread, hoping for fresh food
Hospital sustains the crash
Thousands upon thousands bandaged an open gash

Water recedes, taken all we have like a thief
Destruction beyond belief
Rebuild with family and friends in unity
Grace and love will save our community

I Can See for Miles

Galloping across savanna woodlands
Eating at the top, I stand
Tasty morsels of white, yellow flowers
Swirling my tail like a flyswatter

Camouflage coat so you cannot see
Patterns so unique to me
Humming, grunting in the herd
Graceful beauty speaks to the birds

Moving my stilts with flexibility
Peaceful calm of passivity
Revealing innocent vulnerability
Gentle aura of femininity

Watching over the plains, awakening kindness
Elevation of the spirit removes blindness
Necking establishing dominance
Folding sticks to kneel, resting consciousness

Shimmering up to gaze the visual field
Seeing your friends revealed
Sliding down reddish-brown neck
Dismounting on the high deck

Face of motherhood, so precious a mood
Cones covered in skin, combative attitude
Black tongue can lick your face from afar
When standing on Christmas tree star

Wander without fear for safety
Towering message of divine, daily
Extinction looms behind
Nature's harmonic balance of no other you will ever find

Ripening

Skin wrinkles slowly
Limbs give way like soft ravioli
Speech slurs, tongue stuck with a C clamp
Muscles cramp
Recollections stay
Grandchildren play
Friends pass, lives crystallize
Gatherings with misty eyes
Enjoying the sunrise
Hearing compromised
Thankful for the birds that fly
Dancing to music, swaying my hips
Sweetness of my mate's lips
Enjoying a juicy steak
Sticking around for potato baked
Opportunities to intercede
Adventures abound, no time to concede
Loneliness tries to apprehend
Having a friend that never ends
Spirit comes in the form of a dove
Tears and laughter, gifts from above
Father that sees all
Saving a place, I recall

Claustrophobic Bubbles

Can't reach the slot
Missed the code, I thought
Try again in the lane
Move forward, start the rain
Am I on the track?
Have to back
Neutral please, confusing
Am I moving?
Here comes the arm
Brushes, swirling alarm
Slappy ribbons of rags thrashing
Soap of multicolors splashing
Will I make it through?
Might get stuck, sinking canoe
I'm sweating, polarizing
Blood pressure's rising
Feels like I'm standing still
Will it break the glass, overfill?
Drowning in bubbles?
Breakthrough from white knuckles
Trusted blower
Dry off slower
Needed a bath
Safe from the wrath
Now it's clean
My four-wheeled machine

Valiant Protectors

I am being robbed
Busted windows by the mob
Graffiti all around
Steal whatever I want, breakdown
Burn down the station
Drive-by at graduation
Murders, executions
Mass shootings
Daily trauma train
Affects the brain
Misconduct, brutality
Civil rights violations, immorality
Miranda warning
Alley court alarming
Handcuffed, beaten, smashing
Sirens and lights are flashing
Reversal of the status quo
Firm compassion is bestowed
Kidnapping children
Civil disorder until then
Enforce the law
Protect property grandpa
Who can I call?
Defunding all
Public safety is lost
At what cost?
Sheriffs, marshals, Mounties
Troopers, rangers, constable, crown these
Detectives, K9, SWAT, new uniforms
Threads of fabric have been torn
Senseless violence on the streets
End the enemy's lawlessness recipe
Community of one to fight the crime
Altogether scrubbing off the slime
Handgun, batons, teargas, rubber bullets
Vans, armored vehicles, fire extinguishers, hook ups

Continued on next page

Shields, water cannons, tasers, flashlights, whistles
Barricades, motorcycles, helicopters, bicycles
New tools needed, protecting society's wedding band
Most important the defibrillator's hand
Divine intervention
For this sacrificial blue group to stand

Mused Whim

Revealing stories, pondering in my heart and mind
Silly things, noble things, nature's time
Realizing many things to be defined
Thousands upon thousands, particles refined

Walking slowly, road shown
Approaching tunnel of the unknown
Adrenaline rush, through my soul
Joyful scenes appear in the memory's scroll

Masters painting human figures having dinner
Attempting to craft again, learned beginner
Only achieved one after another
Pouring out thoughts, to be uncovered

Observing underneath the carpet substrate
Spiderweb of both love and hate
Wishes to change the dates
Illuminating towering heavenly gates

Entering subway train beneath the street
Moving fast without sight from the backseat
Doors slide open, new explanation
Discovering fun filled destination

Continuing my journey to begin
Of rhymes and riddles within
Describing the unseen wind
Pouring out in a mused whim

Broken Love

Feeding from birth, gift from above
Deepest nurturing love
It's lost now, I cry
Where are you? Sadness in my eyes

Asked to draw in school, she's gone away
Picture for this special day
Nothing to say
Sisters in charge, feelings hideaway

Seeing you with other guys
Too young to realize
Home, fighting, screaming, yelling
Hurting darkness consumes our dwelling

Innocence, a broken frontier
No concern for the wounded with fear
No cheerleader, coach, or trainer
Younger years, I won't blame her

Sacred journey almost missed
Took me to the hospital when I was sick
Worked hard all day to feed us fish sticks
New boyfriend, no picnic

Knowing deep down in her heart
I was her special little boy from the start
Tough time in life, then sickness fell
Pray against the curse from hell

I know you love the Lord, I tell
When I see you again I'll spell
Mother's Day card I couldn't draw
Yet your love cared without a flaw

Child's Play

Golden crunch beneath my feet
Adjusting skin, loss of heat
Chill in the air
Carved orange faces stare

End harvest time forecast
Remembering those who passed
Will-o-the-wisps, Stingy Jack legend adapted
Danse macabre first outfitted enacted

Playful searching discovered
A wardrobe of another
Soul cakes lead the trend
Irish and Scottish start ahead

Roaming the misty night
Mumming, guising causing fright
Little ghouls and goblins come to be fed
Or a jovial trick instead

Now my bag is full
Sugar rush, a mouthful
Innocence child's play
Celebrating this holiday

Gladly Pay You Tuesday

Germany or the US
Travel by immigrants
Patents for the grinder
NY Delmonico restaurant finder
On the menu
Dr. Salisbury war venue
Cows and cowboys
Refrigerated cars deployed
Corruption in processing
Erie County Fair commenting
St. Louis World's Fair burst
Castle the first
Speedee then Ronald
Drive-through modeled
Fast and cheap
Others began to sweep
Older boy now exists
With a new double twist
Then the King
Goliath of a story fling
Millennium Falcon with an olive
Globalization lot of
Pat me down
Thick, thin, plump, or round
Flaming gas, charcoal brown
Rare, medium, well done, 160° Fahrenheit
Jump on top, green, yellow, white
Covered with a waterfall of red
Placed on the bed
Cover me with a sheet
Tasty, juicy treat
Famous picnic friend
With fries, a scrumptious dividend

Shared Presence

Sit with me
Watch the sunrise
Walk with me
Garden path, mesmerize

Place your feet with me
In the gentle stream
Smell the fragrance with me
Of the flower's dream

Taste the juice with me
Of the grape
Climb with me
On rocks of escape

Run with me
Up, up the hill, fulfill
Eat with me
Your desired meal

Read with me
Verses you love
Stare at clouds with me
Voice from above

Rest with me
As the sun sets
Fall asleep with me
Share His presence

Special Day

Does the planet observe its time?
Ringing bells and chimes
One more walk around the path
Seems to move awful fast

Mind records it all
Picture albums standing tall
Playing in the sandbox
Cap and gown, buying stocks

Marriage, castle domain, mortgage pay
All day the children play
First new car
Then a Jaguar

All starts to fade away
Colossal blessings, when turned from the alleyway
Gather alone or with some
Reflective time to hear the beating drum

One candle then too plenty
Slice of chocolate, plate empty
Thankful for the joyous presents
For those beautiful daily events

Gift of birth, dodged the sad
Host of many were so glad
That glorious day
Celebrating together at the dancing soiree

What I Didn't Know

Observing minute spec
Calculating observed respect
Developing understanding, unknown
Comprehension in participation, cornerstone

Filling empty vessels, animate
Interpreting the debate
Debriefing reflective feedback
Collaborating out of the backpack

Demonstrating the profound
Generalizing what's been found
Induction, deduction to justify
Analysis, analogy, go verify

Instructional explanation, references spoke
Logical inner change awoke
Comprehensible describing alignment
Knowledge completing the assignment

Imparting reasoning with flexibility
Lectures, seminars, tutorials, plausibility
Communicating in story, telling directions
Interpreting learning connections

Answers to millions of questions
Learning to seek life's lessons
Reasoning computations glow
Knowing what I didn't know

Grab My Hat

Storylines expressed my youth
As I aged became reflective truth
Joyful innocence began
Revolution of sounds took a stand

Lyrics I can listen over and over again
Became my closest friends
Melodies, harmonies like butter bread
Mystery to what was being said

Harmonic language hard to convey
Without expressing the words some way
Singing on our way home from school
Expressing the first innocent love, so cool

King dethroned by hair and boots
Thousands of screaming girly hoots
Two movies of fun I'll never forget
Lads captured our imagination, public threat

Sent home from school, hair too long
Started with these four all along
Greatest writers that transcend
My love for their music will never end

Serenity

Gentle wind turns the book pages
Waves lap the beach as sun sets for ages
Stoplight changes red, no cars at midnight
Single prop plane flies overhead at daylight

Morning fog lifts its shades
Dew blankets the blades
Treetops silently sway
Honey-suckers buzz away

Distant train whistle, hound's voice
Full moon reflected river's choice
Tiny fan rotates a cooling path
Running hot water for a bath

Flower scent awakes
Radio song opens the memory gates
Wave goodbye as they drive away
Saddening silence, wish they could stay

Thankful for the peaceful time we've had
Discard noisy, chaotic world that's mad
Breathing in refreshing air
Serenity's voice you can't compare

My Turf

Not safe to walk home, fear is happening
Hear a voice, I'm strapping
Pick up the pace, not my party
Hey, are you dirty?
You holding down, homeboy
Grandma's house a refuge, enjoy
Thirst monsters two blocks away
Five-o throwaway, cast away, went astray
Torn screen, broken door, smashed window
Landlord ups the rent, bingo
Trying to be a buster, cool
Join our school, will protect, we rule

Your turf is small
Need to get out if I must crawl
This reality is forsaken
Boy, you must be mistaken
Got loads of cash, pay no tax
It's dirty, creating infectious tracks
Bullets are flying
Numb to death, no crying
Businesses are closed, kill zone
Streetlights standing alone
Except for the poisonous stash
Broken neighborhood murder's whiplash

You haven't heard the word
Reconstructing within transferred
Not accepting the poverty lies
Build a new domain enterprise
Inner courage without a tray eight
What Martin Luther called the bate
Shedding violence, peaceful mandate
Executing the insurgence of hate
Listen to the Creator's whisper surf
Giving control to my decimated turf

Up, Up, and Away

Waiting for a windy day
So my fabric with a tail can play

Holding on to the middle strand
With a ball in my hand

Running as fast as I can
Releasing the string upon demand

Up, up, up, pull it tight
Catch the air with all your might

Sways to the left, sways to the right
Daddy, Daddy, it's taking flight

Release more string to get some height
Look, it's so high, reflecting the sun's light

Now let it fly with the birds
Joyous afternoon, can't express with words

Scent

Discovering underpass
Smelling the green grass

Hoping to find its hole
Looking down below

Dig, dig, dig up the dirt
Senses alert

Fooled again, back door
Now a state of war

Turning into a tyrannosaur
That gopher's done for

Called in for lunch
Back to chop and crunch

Catch the scent
Stopped by the fence

Tired out, laid down
Surrender to the petting of my crown

Freedom to Choose

Some have no choices, shadowy ravine controlled
Freedom's eyes darkened by a blindfold
Blessed for Liberty's outstretched hand
Value self-determined course, action plan
Counterfeits smashing against precious pillar, standing tall
Human right, woven thread, the fabric shawl

Eighteen marching starts, knowledge to be confident
Registered citizen, take an oath, ennoblement
Validating my participation, opinions—can they be heard?
Be informed against lying spin, truth blurred
Issues and views, alignment I choose
Freedom's truthful wand to infuse

Paper, lever, punch card
DRE optical controversy, discarded in the backyard
270 not the popular stagecoach pathway
100 deliberate and prestigious, can we say?
Powers of advice and consent keynote speech
Justices, judges, treaties, ambassadors, who can we impeach?

435 legislation, legislation, Godly decisions
Pray earnestly for divine visions
Cherish upper and lower body
Betting on the horse or jockey
Fleshly parts of bicameral machine
Drinking from the poisonous lobbyist canteen

24th Amendment, Act of 65, Article 1
Balance of power, history won
Unity of 535 to understand the treasure at hand
World's watching as we battle dictatorship's stand
Never give up the freedom to choose
The day we do, democracy will lose

Awakened

Maidens' purity the messenger spoke
Troubled by the words evoke
Fear be gone I say
Chosen this day

Delivery of the young
Overshadowed light from high has begun
Garden chair will never rot
Planting seed in the flower pot

May it be a new tree
Tell a friend, foresee
Inside burst forth jubilation
Shyness recognized confirmation

Days after days after days
Demolish the prominent gaze
Extinguished high places, golden fountain
Gathered quietness up the mountain

Satisfied the famished drought
Golddiggers cast out
Recalling being compassionate, fervently
Repeatedly, endlessly, eternally

Lost and Found

Long to hold an embrace
Love that won't escape

Your mine forever now
You erased the inner darken cloud

Traveling timeless, haunting miles
Captured back your sweet inner child

Long to hold an embrace
Love that won't escape

Drank until I couldn't see the road
Loneliness griped my faith, a condemning heavy stone

Crashed at homes I didn't know, thought I died
Stumble down the roadway path to find my ride

Long to hold an embrace
Love that won't escape

Then one day it all came back
Found myself sitting on the railroad track
Jump the train to find my way home
Broke the glass and cleared the smoke
Emptied my backpack

Ohhh, ohhh, came the grace
Ohhh, ohhh, came the grace
Ohhh, ohhh, came the grace
Ohhh, ohhh, came the grace

Continued on next page

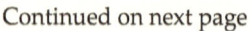

Brighter than the brilliant sun, I became totally overcome
Scent strong, intoxicating my whole being, becoming numb

Porcelain shape with golden strands, luscious red, stares that fed
Piece that was missing, bleeding time, my heart fulfilled, newlywed

Long to hold an embrace
Love that won't escape

Divine connection I must've had
Gave me my mate and took away the sad

Testify to the overcoming of the black, poisonous soul
I'm now drenched with love that consoles

Long to hold an embrace
Love that won't escape

Ohhh, ohhh, came the grace
Ohhh, ohhh, came the grace
Ohhh, ohhh, came the grace
Ohhh, ohhh, came the grace

Street Sketcher

So many street corners
Dim, shattered lights, mourners
Exited prepaid subway
Trapped in the alleyway
Climb up the fire escape
Home cold steel step, friction tape

Dim-n-daddy, dim-n-daddy, dim-n-daddy dew
Dim-n-daddy, dim-n-daddy, dim-n-daddy threw

Tears falling slow
Garbage can below
Sirens passing, maintain
Lightbulb relieves the pain
Rush blinds my mind
Score is tied, it's overtime

Dim-n-daddy, dim-n-daddy, dim-n-daddy dew
Dim-n-daddy, dim-n-daddy, dim-n-daddy threw

Music from an open window
Subdue ray of a bright, escape limbo
Still small voice, clearness
Entering of the enormous
Flushing the poisonous thief
Singing fire flashes, incinerate unbelief

Dim-n-daddy, dim-n-daddy, dim-n-daddy dew
Dim-n-daddy, dim-n-daddy, dim-n-daddy threw

Continued on next page

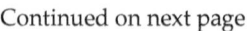

Captured by the hope catcher
No longer the street sketcher
Broke the paws that ate my flesh
My soul and true inheritance, refreshed
Giving thanks for the divine intervention
Testifying at the I AM convention

Dim-n-daddy, dim-n-daddy, dim-n-daddy dew
Dim-n-daddy, dim-n-daddy, dim-n-daddy threw

Whatever I Have, Wherever I Am

Woke by
Sunrise delight
Thankful for
Pain at night
Giving gratitude
Protective covering
Into the land
Of new discovery

Mighty hope
Never abandoned
My cherished
Companion
Amazing colors
Surround my head
In the dark kingdom
Seeking light never ends

Dance, prance
Swirl around
Whispers and songs
Of the King's crown
Peace contentment
Laughter and joy
At sunset's evening ploy

My Name

Designer I know
Who sees all below
Almighty embrace
Eternal grace
Provider of needs
Master planting seeds
Healer of disease
Banner high above the trees
Consuming fire refining
Peace ever-shining
Chariot of hosts
Rock-supporting golden posts
Shepard protecting the flock
Refuge under the boardwalk
Shield from incoming
Fortress drumming
Strength beyond measure
Judge, eternal thrasher
Hope never denied
Always there beside
Father, nurturing our needs
Truth given to succeed
Joy overflowing
Love, ever knowing

New Ride

Audit of my heart
Cathartic start
Lonely trails behind
Drifting through memories of my mind

Never seen before this age
Refreshing time to engage
Scenic adventure with some dismay
Pain, pleasure, construct an archway

Monocular to speak to others
Roads crossed to have their druthers
Softly spoken, insurgent's wind
Healing encouragement, thick skinned

Broken loose the particles of decay
Reformed by the potter's clay
Crackpot for so many days
Reformation in so many ways

Gloom and doom have been nullified
New highway inside
Must confide
Jesus is my ride

Cloak of Love

How did I get here?
My side is sore, I can barely hear
Concrete's cold, my stomach's empty
Looking out my makeshift tent of plenty

Blankets draped over my shopping cart
Where is my home? My kids alone, broken heart
Needing the glorious poison to regain
One last time just to maintain

Soup kitchen is a block away
Pack my things and stumble that way
Foul odor in the line I'm in
Need a bath to relieve the itch of my skin

Raise my sign and extend my can
Dollar, please help me stand
Got enough to make a score
Now I'm back on the concrete floor

Choked by the exhaust smoke
In Land of Plenty, I might have a stroke
Crawling on my hands and knees
From this blackness under the trees

Here comes an extended hand
Bringing back to the Promised Land
United with my kids and wife
Renounce this cursed way of life

Restored my faith and sanity
Giving back damaged humanity
Homeless, starving, forsaken
Cloak of love, awaken

No Help Needed

At my age some things
Need to be shared, like a bird's broken wing

It's so dumb
Probably, share with another chum

When my legs don't work it takes a toll
Physically bend my leg to fit through the hole

Happens to be the wrong one
Start over now, I'm having fun

Toenail claws catch the rim
Pull them up, I can't win

Try to release the snag
Now, a cramp in my leg

Rather embarrassing feat
Glad to be alone so you can't witness this treat

Up they go, now I stand
Glad they've got a stretchy waistband

Sit back down to finish the job
Compression socks, so my feet won't throb

Pull up the second covering
As I start muttering

Remembering I'm not alone
Thankful I finished the job on my own

Potato Soup

Staring at a blank page, my thoughts fade away
Wondering what I can say

The snow is slightly falling
Winter on the doorstep calling

On this same kind of day
Wrote a poem in a small café

Over potato soup with my mate face to face
It was cozy warm by the fireplace

Peaceful, romantic, sipping caffeine
Looking through paned glass, gentle river scene

Engraved a memory, precious jewel, ironclad
Such sweet moments the presence had

Staring out the kitchen window
Remembrance of that day continued

Heartfelt love we felt together
In the small café in November

Thanksgiving

In grade school
Feeling like a fool
Drew around my hand in red
Colored feathers and wattle underneath the head
All were joyous and happy
Lonely for my displaced mommy and daddy
Knowing we had little or no bread
Awesome family meal was dead

On this celebration loneliness was the gravy
Heartache, depression, it seems so crazy
Next year invited to the relatives
Distant family gathers, seating preferences
To the basement we ate
Aunts, uncles whispered insidious hate
Nowadays when I look back
Pain and sorrow were a temporary attack

Highlighted on that day's celebration
Giving way to wisdom's emancipation
Being thankful for all that was given
For a new, loving family that has risen
Today that turkey drawing is hung on the wall
Expressing love for the lost, hungry, and small
Child's simple gift I recall
For God's grace has covered us all

Around the Meal

Macy's Parade, then best dog show
Preparing for all to come, shovel the snow
Ice forming on the lake
Young crew appears, with skates
Table set with colorful plates
Centerpiece and candles lit
Sharing stories and laughter abounds
Ones that are distant, a Zoom sound
Gather together, such a precious gift
Never take for granted, you may be missed
Share a prayer of thanksgiving all around, check list
From the oven, smells of turkey and ham
Mashed potatoes with gravy thick, bam
Sweet potatoes buttery, cranberry delight
Hot toasted muffins, roasted asparagus, sit tight
Fruit salads and cherry Jell-O
Stuffing, stuffing, stuffing, top with marshmallows
Pumpkin pie, spritz of cream, coffee brew
Out to the bonfire with the crew
Hockey puck flying through
Ice is thick by the shore
Careful not to go out too far
Relax back in my lounge chair
Football game, traditional sight
Loosen my belt and say good night

Oh, I forgot, we did breakfast, brunch—morning delight

Overtime

Lunch with a friend
Tales of the musical weekend
Sharing good old times about everything
Also what the future may bring

How to stop time?
New names add to the family line
Love these afternoon greetings
Get in touch with some inner feelings

Catch up on the news of the day
Make the best of it, soon will fade away
Sandwich and fries, pot of coffee
Glad I retired being bossy

Anxious to retreat to a new spot
Coordinating all the pieces, becoming distraught
How to sell so your heart won't rot?
On the horizon a new adventure, a forethought

Up from the table we stand
Shoulder hug and shake hands
Buddies that seem aware
About a world that doesn't care

Back to the place where we were
Before we took time to escape the blur
Stay in touch, call for the next lunchtime
Visit longer creating an overtime rhyme

Let's Toast

Eggroll, pot of tea
Hot mustard, nostrils free
Care for our mother
Choosing palette of colors
Stroke of words to others

Living in the cloak of time
Dividing segments of your mind
Attempting creative expressions of the soul
Adventurous journey entering cruise control
Hidden pieces becoming whole

Transforming a polished jewel
Fastened into a crown of renewal
Diverse language begins to speak
Etched character becomes complete
Nuances emerge upbeat

Discussion over breaking of bread
Vital pulse to relationship's thread
Laughter over present times and past
How long will our bodies last?
Hip, knee, heart, mind steadfast

Relaxing to the camera's view
New panther breaking through
Construct continuum flight
Into the cold wintry white
Ride home and say good night

Somebody Lad

Somebody lad
Gathering in a somebody land
Sharing with everyone firsthand

Knows exactly what to say
Navigates his journey way
Seeking all of humanity, astray

Hearing what's been said
Don't be misled
Capturing hearts, spiritually dead

Eyes that can't see
Ears that can't hear
Opened, never to disappear

Grasp my hand
Archway of tenderness stands
Entering the kingdom who understands

Somebody lad
Gathering in a somebody land
Sharing with everyone firsthand

Silent Whispers

Silent whispers beneath the crease
Shouting out to be released
Passion's hand brings relief

Running down the orchard's path
Jubilant laughter unmasked
Loneliness and fear take a bath

Vaporizing unmentionable flashes
Enjoying simple, solemn, fresh glasses
As the darkness turn to ashes

Gathered into the arms of stillness
Healing the depressive illness
Rocking in the cradle of forgiveness

Bursting forth the light that shines
Joyous breaking undefined
Stampede of horses turn grapes to wine

Drink to the celebration
Astonishing, reborn creation
Of the miraculous Spirit's manifestation

Gift of Time and Space

Millions of words I'll never use or understand
As I write some with my hand
Once they're out the door
Read by someone, admired or placed in the drawer
Will they be heard evermore?

A story once spoke
Pages and pages alive that evoke
Volumes upon volumes put on the shelf
Fade away, collecting dust, a thing in itself
Preserved in a time capsule by a colorful elf

Rhymes and riddles my tongue pronounce
Things I see, hear, feel, and imagine, I announce
Joyful times I ponder as I keep the pace
Gift to occupy everyplace
Summarizing the human race

So, if you link up to these words
Try not to be too discouraged
Allow abbreviations in your mind
Of subtle messages so sublime
Peaceful words may dissipate undefined

Cherish the reading, as you breathe
Conductor shouts all aboard! Who believes?
Watching the train as it leaves
Say goodbye to your hiding place
Of the gift of time and space

I Feel Good, Dada Dada Dada Dah

One hundred again
My most cherished friends
Joyous time, when we meet with the pen
Saying goodbye as others might read
Stories, tales of inner adventures, planting seed

Revealing pain, happiness, joy, hopeful finish
Walking across the broken bridge
Climbing to the top of a mountain ridge
Gathering memory stones, we can't see
Revealing inner spirit to believe

Homeless, abandoned, addicted, hungry
Senseless violence, city decay, power of prayer to bring an end
Healing the cancer of my friend
Laughter's medicine of silly things
Intimate love with soaring wings

Animals with necks so high
Moving shells, thousands of years verify
Flying masters of the air
Cousins of the beautiful wings of flair
King of the dark blue, we become scared

Rhythms of a musical composer
Garden, canvas, swirling wind, need a bulldozer
Explorers of outer space, songs of the street band
Keepers of our earth and land
Toasted bread and staple friend

Silk covering for our bed, communicating device
Aging with memories' time, resting in paradise
Large ovals float on by
Poked by a fork, say goodbye
Bicycle ride, looking through a glass of time

Continued on next page

Listen to light in the silly world
It's a wish, new dance, a swirl
Pilot asking a magical lady about earth's love
Destructive winds, ocean waves, grace from above
Mother lost, car wash of my lady love

Speeding red truck, blue let you cross
Soldier returning home, feeling lost
Hamburger with barbecue sauce
Celebrating your special day
Learning and teaching every which way

Musical group I adore
Serenity out the backdoor
Freedom to choose, a gopher's scent
Birth of the lamb, poverty's street tent
Forgiveness, turning to rust all I have
Names that make me glad

Moment at the small café
Celebration got lost halfway
Abundance on that future day
Lunch, dinner, movie with a friend
Lad that found his way

Presence of the Holy Spirit's claim
Crafting words to articulate fame
Glad to have welcomed you into my house
As I rearrange and add new furniture about
Sharing faith, conversations, thoughts as I bow out

Enjoy expressing so many things in life
Devotional adventure, affection for my wife
Humanity's existence of love proclaimed
Sometimes an interpreter of God's earthly domain
Rejoice and be glad for the next walk again

About the Author

Jeffrey Krueger was born in Milwaukee, Wisconsin, in 1952. He grew up on the northside of Milwaukee in the housing project known as Westlawn. After his parents divorced, at the age of eleven he moved into his grandmother's home in Wauwatosa, a suburb of Milwaukee, and graduated from Wauwatosa East High in 1970. Continuing his studies, he attended Layton School of Fine Arts, Milwaukee; University of Milwaukee, Wisconsin; and the University of Minnesota, Minneapolis, spanning the years from 1970–1978.

He has been involved in the entertainment business for over fifty years. After arriving back from the Woodstock Festival in 1969, he produced his first outdoor concert in 1970.

In the late '70s and early '80s he was lead singer of the music group the American Pilots, writing and producing the demo LP Heart Notes. *For a short time, he became an entertainment consultant in the Twin Cities area, producing performances of Chuck Berry, Eddie Money, Savoy Brown, Traffic, Todd Rundgren, The Baby's, Ricky Nelson, Tommy James & the Shondells, Kiki Dee, Hall & Oates, Peter Tosh, Herman's Hermit, and Poco.*

In 1983, he founded the country music festival WE Fest, Detroit Lakes, Minnesota, one of the largest festivals in the nation. For twenty-eight years, he was at the helm as president of WE Fest, until his semiretirement in 2010. He produced shows of the who's who in country music, to just mention a few: Dolly Parton, Johnny Cash, Willie Nelson, Waylon Jennings, Tim McGraw, Kenny Chesney, Miranda Lambert, Kid Rock, Keith Urban, Carrie Underwood, George Strait, Little Big Town, Brad Paisley, Blake Sheldon, Eric Church, Rascal Flatts, and Taylor Swift.

After rededicating his life to his Christian faith at a Promise Keepers event in Minneapolis in August 1997, he launched a Christian festival called Spirit Fest. It included six stages and over thirty musical acts and speakers per day, including artists Michael W. Smith, Amy Grant, Steven Curtis Chapman, Third Day, Newsboys, Point of Grace, Skillet, Big Daddy Weave, Delirious, Phil Driscoll, Ragamuffin Band, 4Him, and a host of others.

He created a fundraiser called the Family Needs Fund, a nonprofit organization. It was designed and dedicated to assisting the crises and circumstantial needs of families. For the last eighteen years, the charity has been active in helping families with their basic needs and continues today.

In addition, he produced two live musical worship CDs for the Power of God Band, Delivered and POG Live. Both CDs were sold and utilized as a fundraiser for families in need. All the proceeds were donated to the FNF charity.

He shared his written testimony on how God saved his life, healing him from the addiction to drugs and depression. He witnessed the healing power of the Holy Spirit, guiding him throughout his life, and it is reflected in some of his poems.

During his retirement, he consulted a small Christian music festival called Hope Fest, a fundraiser for the homeless, hungry, and lost.

For the last thirty-seven years, he has been a devoted husband, father, and grandfather to four children and nine grandchildren. He defeated cancer with God's healing power, became a full-time farmer in Hardwood Hills Vineyard, a reclaimed wood-furniture maker, and inventor of E-Z Stack (e-zstack.com).

Jeffrey began to explore writing to challenge himself in 2004. He finished his first writing, a screenplay called The Maestro, *in 2009, and at present is transposing it into a novel. He continued writing his autobiography,* Volume 1 Cause and Effect: A Life's Journey, The Younger Years, *and* Volume 2 Cause and Effect: Light Invades the Darkness. *He finished his first published book of poems on December 29, 2021:* Dad's 100 Poems, Riddles, and Songs in 100 Days.

He started his second book on March 20, 2022, and finished on December 3, 2022: Dad's 100 Poems, Songs, and Riddles Within, *which is similar to his first book of poems. They range from sometimes silly subjects—a toaster, fork, toilet paper, stapler—to more serious reflections of life, aging, preserving the land, addiction, a Savior, tornadoes, hurricanes, senseless violence, the human condition. Also recording daily moments of the surroundings and habitat including certain animals and insects. Some are commentaries on subjects such as freedom, war, and the environment. Many of his poems are also a reflection of his Judeo-Christian faith, believing in the power of prayer and the healing power of God's Holy Spirit.*

Proceeds from the sale of *Dad's 100 Poems, Songs, and Riddles Within* are donated to the Family Needs Fund, a charity to help families in need.

familyneedsfund@gmail.com
PO Box 885
Detroit Lakes, MN 56501

Other Books by
Jeffrey Krueger

Dad's 100 Poems, Riddles, and Songs in 100 Days